A BOOK
of
BLESSINGS

by
Jan Elkins

with
Anna Elkins

Listening Heart
PO Box 509
Jacksonville, OR 97530 USA
jan@livingwatersmedford.org
ISBN-13: 978-0692516621
ISBN-10: 069251662X

Cover design by Anna Elkins

Printed in the United States of America

DEDICATION

I dedicate this book of blessings to my children, Anna and David. You are my greatest treasure and legacy. Many of these blessings were written directly for you, and all were printed here with you in mind.

CONTENTS

May the Lord, the God of your ancestors, increase you a thousand times and bless you as he has promised!
—Deuteronomy 1:11 NIV

PREFACE

From Jan Elkins:

When I was three years old, my family moved to Chalatenango, El Salvador. It was 1954, and most of that developing, Central American country had no telephones or television. My childhood years were basic, but I've always loved them.

I lived in a world of two languages and two cultures. I loved my Spanish friends and their families. I would visit them and play in tiny adobe, thatch-roofed homes with dirt floors, inhabited by humans and livestock. I also played in homes with *teja* roofs and tiled *salas*. At the time, indoor plumbing in our town was available only in the little home my dad built for us. To this day, I am not fond of outhouses!

It was always too hot to cook, but because of my love for tortillas, I would help make them while on our many visits to neighbors and friends. I loved taking the corn and rolling it on stone until the *masa* was ready. Then I formed thick *gorditas* by hand and cooked them on top of the clay oven in the outdoor kitchen. I was surrounded by lovely, gracious people who lived in poverty and under the rule of a wealthy minority. Despite hardships, those tropics brimmed with beautiful landscapes and people.

I did not grow up with an understanding of blessings, other than feeling generally blessed. I was taught that I was blessed the moment I believed in Jesus Christ, who died for me and saved me.

I witnessed much goodness. I also saw oppression, injustice, drunkenness, and murder. In one sense, I lived a life as an outsider in a place that felt like home. When our family first came to Chalatenango, the leading Catholic priest hated us *gringos,* fearing our influence on the community. He did his best to turn as many people as he could against us and to run us out of town. Our neighbors and all those who knew us in town liked us—some even loved us—so the priest tried stirring up dissent with those who came to town weekly from the countryside. From my earliest memories I remember being called a *puta:* prostitute.

Early on, my parents started hearing rumors of an uprising. I remember the night a lynch mob filled our street block. They came chanting, "Death to the Protestants!" They carried rocks, rags soaked in kerosene, and homemade bombs. The regiment of soldiers policing Chalatenango showed up just as the crowd reached the entrance to our home. Using bayonets, the soldiers pushed back the crowds and made them disperse.

Dad built our home across from a medical clinic. I was fascinated with the clinic. It was an open-air building with a few rooms and long verandas. Sometimes, I witnessed machete injuries from serious fights. People arrived hacked up and bleeding, carried in from the countryside in hammocks.

More often, on the cobbled streets, I saw a different kind of pain: men drunk from a night's binge, trying to sleep off the alcohol and the reason they'd consumed it in the first place.

I was drawn to suffering because I was drawn to healing. One of the first expressions of this calling was my interest in that little medical clinic. In sixth grade, I got permission to put on a mask and gown, stand at a patient's side, and witness an operation while the doctor explained every step of the way, using unfamiliar Spanish medical terms.

Afterward, a nurse gave me a tour of the facility. The burn wards, open to the heat and bugs, were hardest to walk through. The smell added to the misery. At a young age, I decided to be part of the healing for the wounded and hurt by becoming a nurse.

I knew I had a heritage from my parents, who brought our family to a foreign land to bring the Good News of God's love, grace, and mercy. I knew I was blessed and at some point, I understood that our family had a calling to be a blessing.

Though I never entered the medical field, my two sisters, a brother-in-law, and a nephew did. But I also became a healer, by the authority and power of Jesus Christ. Since 1981, my husband, Garris, and I have been blessed to pastor three churches and to serve, support, mentor, and minister to leaders in the United States and abroad. We have witnessed God give real and lasting healing. It starts from the inside. Spirit, soul, and body are completely intertwined and cannot be separated: three in one...and all have to be addressed in order to thrive.

In my years of mentoring, coaching, raising a family—and simply interacting with humanity—I have learned the power of blessings. God's plan of redemption includes blessings of supernatural favor. He imparts His unlimited goodness upon us. His blessings are for the here and now—His Kingdom here on earth, as it is in Heaven. Blessings have been significant from the Old Covenant right into the New Covenant.

To be *blessed* means *to be fully satisfied*. Blessings are not dependent upon favorable circumstances; they are sourced in God and in the joy that comes from being saved and indwelt by Jesus Christ.

Jesus became my Savior when I was a little girl, but I did not yield to His Lordship and entrust myself to the only One who satisfies until 1979, when I was raising children of my own. At that time, I encountered the Living God in a deep way—and that was just a beginning. When I look back over my life, I can see how God pursued me and how He revived, restored, and released me into His grand purposes. All this was not only for me but also for all those I love—and the untold number of people He loves and blesses through them.

I bless you with a heart to receive these blessings.

The Lord's blessing is our greatest wealth. All our work adds nothing to it!—Proverbs 10:22 TLB

From Anna Elkins:

When I was in the first grade, I was the victim of bullying. I would come home from school in tears. I remember my mother leading me through prayers of forgiveness for the girl who was tormenting me. That was hard enough. Even harder was blessing the very person who was responsible for the pain! But I did it.

Today, I am grateful beyond expression for my mother's lesson. Now, when someone says or does a hurtful thing—by intention or accident—I respond in the opposite spirit. I want my heart's default to be one of blessing. I counter anger with blessings of peace, vindictiveness with justice, self-absorption with self-less love. It's not always easy, but it's habit.

I am so glad to be helping my mother put this book together. I know the power of blessings—both as the giver and receiver of them.

May we all bless and be blessed.

INTRODUCTION

All the testimonies of God's faithfulness, goodness, promises, and blessings are blessings for us. All of them. And not only for our generation but also for those who come after us. He wants to partner with us to increase awareness of His presence among us.

Of course, the focus is on God and not just the promise of blessings. Wisdom, knowledge, and prophetic revelations are signs pointing to the One who is the Promise. Our goal is intimacy with God.

We *become* a blessing. We no longer just bless our friends and family. We bless our enemies. We bless those who hurt and wound us, mock and fight against us. The wonder of the Cross of Jesus Christ and His reconciling redemption is so magnificent, it can overcome all evil. The power of a blessing is greater than the power of a curse. Light always overcomes darkness.

A few years ago, a friend gave me a set of audio CDs of scriptural blessings. I listened to them off and on during a five-hour car trip. Looking back, I can see how hearing those words inspired me. Even though I haven't listened to those CDs again, they made a subtle course adjustment within me— realigning and renewing my mind.

I started seeing God's Word in a new way. My prayers began to turn into blessings—or ended in blessings. I began writing Scriptures in blessing form and sending them as prayers for Garris or my kids or friends.

I love releasing the impartation of God's heart of love through blessings of invitation, declaration, and proclamation.

At one point, Garris and my daughter, Anna, asked if I would consider gathering some of these blessings and collecting them in a book. In a family of writers, I found myself inspired and encouraged to do so. Anna is our resident poet, and she helped me to craft these blessings for easy reading and remembering.

The Scriptures I used are mostly life verses or passages that have forged our family's journey. The Holy Spirit also highlighted a few of the Scriptures to me while I was assembling these blessings.

The Old Testament Scriptures that express God's heart and passion reveal Him the same yesterday, today, and forever. I have approached these passages from our New Covenant position—where we stand today. God is just and loves justice, as do we. The laws of God are good, but the human race was unable to fulfill their requirements. Only Jesus the Messiah did not break God's law of love, and He fulfilled all of its requirements for us.

The cost and punishment of every act of rebellion

and missing the mark was paid in full at the Cross. We do not live under judgment. Breaking the law won't separate us from God anymore. Because we said *yes* to His saving grace, our sin will never come between Him and us. At salvation, we are cleansed, fully forgiven, and made complete. Everything pertaining to life is given to us, upfront.

The impartation of a blessing not only calls us forward into God's promises over us, it also reminds us of our eternal standing: no longer separated by our weakness and failings, but forever reconciled and under the fountain of God's favor.

A phrase from a pastor friend has stuck with Garris and me for twenty years: *You are. And you are becoming (experiencing, realizing, living out) who you already are.*

The blessings in this book are an invitation to respond to God, who pursues you with beauty and love, grace and mercy. You can demand that life give you relief from pain and constantly seek elusive comfort (without God you will always be dissatisfied). Or, you can live to know God. I encourage you to face the thirst of your soul and be quenched.

When you read these blessings, keep the eyes of your heart open. Look and listen for instruction, correction, encouragement, etc. God always longs for you to hear Him. He is listening to you.

Each blessing is based on one or more Scriptures, and I noted those. I wrote the blessings by paraphrasing verses in *The Message* and the *New American Standard Bible* and weaving them together.

I encourage you to speak or read these blessings over yourself, your family, your friends—anyone. I found that even strangers accept my invitation to bless them.

Remember that there is usually preparation time before any promise is fulfilled. Our obedience to what God asks of us is an act of *love*. *Patience* is the rare and costly gem purified under pressure, and *hope* is the sure and secure gold setting framing it.

In the end, we want to become and experience who we *are:* brilliant and valiant in the waiting. We want to keep our hearts and hands open to Holy Spirit. Patience matures us so that we won't experience any lack, according to James 1:4.

For any and all promises yet to be fulfilled, I stand with you in hope for that sure thing, as yet unseen.

So take courage! For I believe God! It will be just as he said!—Acts 27:25 TLB

PART I:
BLESSINGS FOR DAILY LIVING

Blessing of Peace
Isaiah 26: 3-4, 7-9, 12

In the Name of Jesus Christ,
    I bless you with a greater level
    of faithfulness and steadfastness
    because you have experienced again and again
    the steadfast, faithfulness of God.

I bless you with such a steadiness of mind
    that you will not quit.
May you depend on God and keep at it,
    knowing that in God you have a sure thing.

I bless you with seeing how God takes a rough path
    and levels it so that your feet are steady and sure.
May you be content and unhurried,
    enjoying the path, immersed in presence.

He has a plan to give you success,
    by using failure *for* you, not against you.
He blesses you and stands with you,
    whether you are doing badly or well.

I bless you with celebrating God and His work in you:
    with being so blessed
    that you are filled and satisfied.
I bless you in the night watches
    as your soul longs for God,
    as your spirit reaches out to Him.

Because God's decisions are on display,
   and everyone can learn how to live rightly,
   may you bless your enemies with eyes to see God.
May He get their attention so they can witness
   His mercy, splendor, and zealous love.

I bless you with a God-ordered, peaceful, whole life
   and the realization that the more life
   you receive from Him,
   the more glory you display—
   increasing your capacity
   to accommodate more life!

Blessing of Holy Living
James 5:16; I John 1:5-10, 2:1-2; James 4:6-10

James 5:16 has been a life Scripture since 1979, when Garris and I were baptized in the Holy Spirit and simultaneously made a decision to allow Jesus full Lordship over us. It has been one of the most powerful promises to live our lives by: no secrets, no hiding in the dark. As we confess our faults to one another and pray for each other, we are healed.

I bless you, in the Name of Jesus Christ,
    with experiencing, becoming,
    and understanding who you already are:
    a child of God.

You are. And you are becoming
    who you already are.

    You are forgiven.
    You are pleasing.
    You are complete.
    You are loved.
    You are holy.

You no longer strive to be holy.

Live holy, with nothing hidden.
You have been redeemed and reconciled;
    you have been given everything
    pertaining to holiness.
May you live each day in the light,

confessing your faults to God
and to one another.
There is no power for holy living,
unless you live in the light;
sin's power is refueled in the darkness.
Pray over each other—declare forgiveness
and healing.
The effects of your sin,
and the sin of others against you,
are washed off.

I bless you with the will to tell others
the truth about yourself.
I bless you with the will to live in openness—
may trust be restored.
I bless you with repentance and forgiveness,
releasing God's gift of grace
to rebuild relationships.

You are not trapped in darkness;
you have been born of light.
Don't hide in the dark—
don't tolerate sin,
don't try to manage your sin.

If you have given Satan a legal right
to defeat you in the darkness, remember:
you have been delivered out of darkness.
May you submit to God; resist the devil,
and he will run from you.

You have been made holy:

you know the power of sin,
you will not minimize sin,
you acknowledge your inability to deal with sin,
you know you can live in the light.

May you love walking in the light,
staying face to face with Jesus.

He invites you:

Run to me,
run to the light,
run with me.

Blessing of Strength

Psalms 28:6-9

I bless you with an impartation of the Holy Spirit,
    in the Name of Jesus Christ.
I bless you with the Lord's strength
    in unresolved issues,
    in points of crisis,
    in the strain of confusion,
    in the heaviness of burden,
    in the sorrow of loss.
I bless you with might, knowledge, and wisdom.
May Love infuse you,
    cascade over you,
    go before you and walk beside you.
Receive God's new mercies this day.

I bless you with patience when listening for guidance,
    with hearing clearly and precisely.
May you take the right, first step and move forward
    with a willingness to quickly obey.

God's heavenly shield surrounds you.
Even if it feels like you are alone,
I declare what God has decreed:

> *I have your back.*
> *I surround you,*
> *and I am in your midst.*

God is your strength and shield.

I bless you with entrusting yourself to Him.
May your heart break open
    to the colors and hues of new life.
I bless you with songs of deliverance and joy.

Blessing of Fathers
Psalm 68:5-6; Matthew 13:52

In the Name of Jesus Christ,
    I bless you with a spirit of adoption.
God is a Father to the fatherless.
I bless you with encountering Him.
No earthly father can fully
    provide what you need
    and what you were created for.
I bless you with discovering who you really are
    in relation to Abba Father.
He gives you your identity;
    you were created uniquely in His image.
He provides all you need—
    spiritually, emotionally, physically.
He provides safety and security.

Your Father is a good judge.
You were created for justice.
Where there has been injustice,
    unfairness, delays, shattered hopes,
    I bless you with ten-fold restoration.
May you be convinced of Abba's
    intentions, character, and heart.
He has a plan and a future for you.
He is just in all His ways.

Your Father makes a home for the lonely.
I bless you with great comfort and healing
    in your Father's gaze,

in your Father's embrace,
in your Father's love.

I bless you with spiritual fathers—
heroes of the faith,
used by Holy Spirit to touch your life.
May you be impacted by writers
old and new who are disciples
of the Kingdom of Heaven.
They are like the head of a household—
a fathering imprint of knowledge and wisdom,
bringing out of their treasures anything you need,
exactly when you need it,
and imparting it to you.

I bless you with fathers
who would mentor and coach you,
who listen well and provide a safety net.
I bless you with encouragers to celebrate
with you and inspire you,
to weep with you and comfort you.
I bless you with a place to call home—
with a father, mother, and family
who open their hearts and doors to you—
a community of faith to love you.
May you reciprocate in like manner.
May you receive a spirit of adoption
and risk belonging to others.

Your Father leads you out from captivity
into prosperity,
from fear into love,

from offense to forgiveness,
from sickness into health,
from destitution to plenty.
Only the rebellious dwell in a parched land.
I bless you with a humble heart,
softened and willing
to entrust yourself to your good Father.

Blessing of Wisdom
Proverbs 17:27; Proverbs 2:6; Isaiah 50:4-5

I bless you, in the name of Jesus Christ,
    with the knowledge of your Creator
    and with understanding breathed
    by the Holy Spirit.

May you speak sparingly
    and respond with calmness of spirit,
    inspired by great confidence in your Source
    and His creative power through you.

Be awakened each morning
    with opened ears to hear,
    taught by the Spirit of the Living God.
May you not turn away and rebel.
I bless you with a staying power
    rather than a desire to escape
    or to fight and force your way forward.
I bless you with obedience to follow through.

Be gifted with a God-breathed voice
    to speak a word of hope to the weary:
    a word of encouragement,
    a word of knowledge,
    a word of wisdom,
    a word of prophecy,
    in the right season, in the right way.
I bless you with trust in God's
    power to be made perfect in you.

Blessing of the Overcomer
Romans 8:28-37; James 1:12-18

I bless you with a deeper reliance on a good God.
You have a future and a hope
    not dependent on circumstance.
Your existence matters mightily;
    you have a destiny designed by your Creator
    and a purpose that counts.

May you offer the good, the bad, and the ugly
    issues of life into the hands of God.
If you love Him, give Him permission
    to work for your good.
God is not the one bringing obstacles and adversity.
He is not tripping you up and making you suffer
    in order to strengthen and change you.
He cannot be tempted with evil,
    and He does not tempt you.
I bless you with belief in a Father
    who made a way for you,
    and who has goodness for your every step.

The author of terrible and tragic events—
    who leaves a legacy of death—
    is Satan and his demonic force.
All his chaos, brutality, and betrayal
    is meant to destroy.
There is no purpose or nobility to evil.
The enemy simply wants to destroy
    your place of intended glory.

If he can add injustice, so much the better.
Darkness is the absence of Light;
    evil is the absence of God's love and truth.
May you refuse to be suspicious of God's intentions
    or blame Him for trouble.
I bless you with God's blessings of supernatural favor
    and the impartation of His unlimited goodness.

When trauma and evil occur,
    I bless you with peace.
I bless you with the heavenly wisdom you seek
    to receive the answer to your cry.
May you hide in the secret dwelling place of God
    and make your heart His home.

There will be tribulation in the world,
    but God has overcome the world.

Jesus never attributes to God
    untimely death, demonic oppression, misery,
    human torment, torture, murder, or sin.
Jesus cut short every funeral He attended.
He represents Father God's heart exactly.
He comes and sits down in your mess with you;
    His holy presence fills your space.
His is the first heart to break,
    and He weeps with you.
Jesus does not cause a distressful event,
    but He will be with you in it and respond to you.
He is the Good Shepherd.
I bless you with rescue.

Jesus did not come to judge and condemn you.
Because you said *yes* to His saving grace,
    your sin will never come between you and Him.
He died of a broken heart, feeling alone and forsaken,
    out of compassion and mercy for you.
Jesus identifies with you and your suffering.
I bless you with Light of Love piercing your darkness.

I bless you with discovery of Peace, Himself,
    in your search of good explanations for suffering,
    asking the many *whys*
    as you dig for understanding.
May you deal with true grief.
May you refuse to look for a substitute when lonely,
    refuse to react with self-loathing when you fail,
    refuse to grow bitter at injustice,
    refuse to shut down your emotions,
    refuse to dismiss, deny, or diminish reality.
I bless you with remaining at your post
    and staying present.
I bless you with overcoming.
Ask yourself:

    God, if you are for me, who can be against me?
    With you on my side, how can I lose?

When all hell is breaking loose
    and trouble crouches at your door,
    when you find no real answer to your questions,
    I bless you with the right questions
    to ask of a good God:

God, I am listening: what are you saying?
God, I am looking: what are you doing?
How can I partner with you?
How can I live from a place of promise?
Where is this good place you are leading me to?

I bless you with absolute conviction
that nothing separates you from God's love.

Despite unpleasantness, pain, or agony,
meaning and purpose are found in your response.
You determine whether you remain a victim
or whether you train to be an overcomer.
May your anguish become the entrance
for your greatest breakthrough
and your deepest transformation.
May your present problem
become the key to healing your past
and the catalyst to creative new beginnings.

I bless you with choosing to respond
with love and goodness,
even if circumstances do not change.
May you no longer live for yourself
but for your God and His purposes.
May you be forever freer,
more compassionate,
and bearing the fruits of the Spirit.
I bless you with discovering
your most valuable treasures
in the places of your greatest hurts.
I bless you with living out of Heaven's higher reality

informing your earthly reality.
God is working for your good!

Blessing of Care
Matthew 6:26-34

When any member of the family is going on a trip, we speak blessings over each other. I spoke this blessing over my daughter, Anna, on her trip to Montana.

I bless you with living in God's reality,
    His initiative, His provisions.
He will meet all of your everyday needs.

Pay attention to what He is doing
    right now, and don't be anxious
    about what may or may not
    happen tomorrow.

God will deal with any difficulties
    when they arise.

Don't you think He'll care for you,
    and do the best for you?

Be careless in God's care
    like the birds—
    free from cares,
    free to fly.

Blessing of God's Goodness
Psalm 73

In 1994, a truth was burned into my heart. I heard the phrase, "God is good," something I had read and heard all my life. But this time, it sounded different. Some corner of my heart came into a conscious awareness that I questioned the veracity of what I had just heard. Something rose up in me, and I found it difficult to say, "God is good." If circumstances were not good, how could God be good? Thank God, for sight! That year I settled in my heart the profound truth of God's goodness, took hold of it, and made a decision to never let it go. I was forever changed. The truth does set you free!

I bless you, in the name of Jesus Christ,
    with celebration at the goodness of God,
    even through the disconcerting
    and hard stuff of life.

Your heart can become embittered and envious
    watching how others prosper.
They don't care what God thinks;
    they get away with arrogance and self-promotion.
It is easy to miss seeing God's goodness
    if you are looking at people instead of Him.
May you fix your eyes on Him.

You wonder why you had tried so hard
    to do good...and for what?
You did not see that the others walked

the slippery road of delusions
leading to disaster and terror.
May you discern the true nature of things.

I bless you with an awakening in your spirit—
with settling it in your heart once and for all:
God is good.
God is good all the time.
God is good, and you can trust Him.

I bless you with experiencing goodness.
May you choose to let God's relentless
kindness touch you.
May you be single-visioned,
with an audience of One.

As you learn to make Him your focus,
I bless you with deliverance
from comparison and competition,
and from being self-focused,
which results in arrogance and judgment.
May you respond in the opposite spirit of these
and exude goodness.

Blessing of Quenched Thirst
John 4:10

In the Name of Jesus Christ,
I bless you with an awareness of your thirst.

God asks:

> *Are you thirsty?*
> *I alone can satisfy your thirst.*
> *Without me, you will always be dissatisfied.*
> *You will always long for me.*

May you know the generosity of God
    and who Jesus is.
He gives you fresh, living water.
I bless you with this water—a spring within you,
    gushing like a fountain,
    never running out—
    quenching you,
    that you may never thirst again.

Blessing of Satisfaction
Luke 6:20-26; Matt. 5:3-12

I bless you in the Name of Jesus Christ.
To be blessed is to be fully satisfied.
You are blessed when you have nothing left
    and you come to the end of the road—
    when you are helpless
    and see your spiritual destitution.

May you walk humbly and receive God's grace.
Without humility, you will not see
    any reason to change.
Humility sees the need
    for more love, joy, hope, faith.
To be poor in spirit—humble—
    makes you great.
The humble turn to God and take refuge in Him.

God revives you and dwells with you.
His Kingdom is here and now.
You will be fully satisfied in Him.

You are blessed when you weep,
    convicted of your sin and lostness.
You will be comforted;
    allow yourself to be embraced
    by the One most dear to you.
You will experience joy in the morning.
May you continue to walk in repentance
    and reap unspeakable joy and be full of glory.

You will be fully satisfied in Him.

You are blessed when you are meek.
Meekness demonstrates gentleness in power—
    a virtue birthed from character
    in humility and self-discipline:
    a controlled strength.
You are willing to see yourself as you really are.
You are willing to submit yourself
    to God and His Word.
You will be an heir and obtain
    an inheritance of His promise.
You will be fully satisfied in Him.

You are blessed when you hunger and thirst for God,
    for then you will discover the feast of Heaven.
I bless you with a constant and recurrent nourishment,
    received from being full
    and hungering to be filled again.
You will be fully satisfied in Him.

You are blessed when you are merciful,
    moved by the power of Christ's love,
    and grieving for the needs of others.
You will experience compassion in return—
    expressed in the power of God's love.
You will receive help for the consequence
    of your own sin.
You will be fully satisfied in Him.

You are blessed when you are pure in heart,
    for you will see God.

Experience His purity through continuous cleansing
   from the pollution and guilt of sin.
As you fulfill these previous conditions of blessedness,
   the more pure your heart becomes
   and the more clearly you can see God.
You will be fully satisfied in Him.

You are blessed when you are a peacemaker.
I bless you with experiencing the peace of God
   and with bringing His peace to others.
You are not only a child of God,
   you also show maturity,
   evidenced by your relationship with the Father
   and your likeness to His character.
You will be fully satisfied in Him.

You are blessed when you are persecuted
   for righteousness' sake.
This righteousness belongs to God.
He offers Himself; His righteousness
   is imparted and imputed to you as a free gift.
May you accept God's claims upon your life;
   I bless you with recognition and acceptance,
   with entrusting and submitting yourself to Him.
May you repent of your sin, and receive
   Jesus Christ as your Savior and Lord.
God's standard of righteousness,
   without you having earned it,
   will satisfy God.
In turn, you have reached the highest level
   of blessedness.
You will be fully satisfied in Him.

You are blessed when people mock you
for your belief in Christ—
when they persecute you and speak
evil against you.
The cause of persecution is your loyalty
to righteousness—both to the Righteous One
and to His directives.
May you walk in humility,
willing to suffer persecutions.
Above all, may you acknowledge Christ's Lordship,
by obeying the revealed will of God.
I bless you with gladness despite the struggle—
a direct result of God's grace.
There is a great reward in Heaven reserved
for the righteous.
You will be fully satisfied in Him.

Blessing of Adoration
Psalm 34

In the Name of Jesus Christ,
    bless the Lord at all times.
Tell your soul to look for every chance to bless Him—
    even when things aren't going well.
Speak to your heart:

> *Be fully satisfied in God.*
> *Live and breathe God.*

May your mouth continually speak praise:

> *I will behold the mystery and wonder of God.*
> *Everything in me declares His love and goodness.*

May you seek the Lord
    and be delivered from all your fears.
When you cry out, He hears you
    and saves you out of all your trouble.
The angel of the Lord surrounds you,
    protects you, and rescues you.
May you experience His nearness
    to your broken heart.
I bless you with deliverance.
He saves those who are crushed in spirit.

Those who enact evil are committing slow suicide;
    they hate the good
    and waste their lives in the process.

I bless you with a guard on your heart and lips.
May you turn your back on sin and do good.
May you pursue Him, who is Peace—
　　take hold of Him,
　　embrace Him.

God keeps His eyes on you,
　　listening for any cry of distress.
Followers of God get into trouble,
　　but He is there every time.
May you find refuge in Him;
　　He has redeemed you.
He does not condemn you.

Taste and see the goodness of God.
You are blessed when He is your refuge—
　　you are blessed when you seek Him,
　　you are blessed when you run to Him,
　　you are blessed when you respond
　　in awe and worship.
You will not lack any good thing.

Blessing of Marvelous Faith
Matthew 8:23-26

Matthew 8 has been my key passage of Scripture to describe the Listening Prayer ministry. Only Jesus can reinterpret our past and the lies we believe. Only He can speak to the root cause of our struggle and bring stillness and peace to our being. Where the presence of the Lord is, there is peace. Perfect peace.

I bless you, in the Name of Jesus Christ,
    with the fearlessness of faith.
When you are led into a furious storm
    through no fault of your own,
    I bless you with courage.
This storm came with no warning—
    it was not intercepted,
    it was not prevented.
Jesus is with you
    as the waves crash over you,
    as you experience peril.
Even as you cry out in panic,
    I bless you with remembrance
    of God's faithfulness—
    of His authority and power
    for yourself and the lives of those you love.
I bless you with new insight and boldness.

Jesus got in the boat, and you followed Him.
I bless you with remembering
    who is with you—always,

who just performed great miracles.
Many who were tormented and demonized
    were delivered with a word.
All who were ill were healed.
He is the Messiah who fulfilled Isaiah's prophecy:

    He took away all our illnesses,
    He took away all our diseases.

He is the One you are following.
As Jesus answers your cry—
    as He stills the sea and you are saved—
    may your *wonder* mature into deep trust.

Jesus is not angry at you.
He knows that you are trying to survive.
He knows you are desperate.
He is glad that you call out to Him for help—
    after all, He is your only option.
He is also offering you
    a life free from being terrorized by fear.
When you are delivered from disaster
    and you arrive at your destination,
    where more miracles await you,
    may you also accept His invitation
    to believe more deeply in Him.

I bless you as you rise up
    to full stature in the Holy Spirit.
May you entrust yourself into God's hand
    even when no rescue is apparent.
Be drawn even closer to the heart of God;

be forever transformed.
As your focus shifts from yourself to Jesus,
    may you use this storm with purpose—
    use it to build your faith
    and to practice where to focus your attention.
As you do, I bless you with fearless living.

Jesus spoke to the cause of the storm
    and to the effects of the storm.
At His rebuke, the tempest is quieted;
    at His word, the waves are calmed—instantly.
In His presence there is peace.
I rebuke the root of your fear as you cry out:

> *Jesus, don't you care that I live?*
> *Why are you asleep on the job?*
> *Is my life important to you?*

Identify and rebuke the root cause:
    the lie that no one cares enough to save you,
    the lie that no one cares enough to stand with you,
    the lie that no one will protect you and provide
    what you need.

Listen to Jesus:

> *Be still.*
> *Where I am,*
> *there is peace*

I bless you with calm and more—
    a merry heart emerging after near disaster,

an awe that asks:

Who is this man, Jesus?
Even the winds and waves obey Him!

May you never be the same again!

I bless you as you walk in His delegated authority,
    facing life in His strength and might.
In every dire and even life-threatening circumstance,
    I bless you with a posture of rest—
    even with deep, rejuvenating sleep.
When you are without clarity or assurance,
    I bless you with peaceful living.
Jesus once marveled at a soldier's faith.
May He also marvel at yours.

Blessing of Joy I
Isaiah 12:6

*No English word can sufficiently describe Heaven's
explosive joy. Being blessed with this emotion will open our
eyes and hearts to acquire the taste and ability to experience
even more heavenly joy.*

I bless you with the stunning discovery
    of holy joy in the God who saves.
I bless you with a cry of awe—
    an emotion you have to hear to understand,
    a shout of victory you have to feel.

Shout out with joy!
Cry out: *God is good!*
Cry out: *God cares!*
May the intensity of your emotions
    overflow to reflect the reality
    that you no longer are lost.
God turned His face towards you.
He saves and delivers.
God loves you.
He fills you with hope.

I bless you with explosive joy!

Blessing of Joy II
Psalm 118:24

I often declare this blessing over my day, resetting my vision to Heaven. The list is really much longer than this. Add any word the Holy Spirit wants to impart.

This is the day the Lord has made!
This is the day of His favor.
This is the day of His glory.
This is the day of His peace.
This is the day of His goodness.
This is the day of His provision.
This is the day of His breakthrough.
This is the day of His tender mercies.
This is the day of deliverance and salvation.
This is the day!

May you be so grateful, so thankful—
    looking at life through the lens of the Spirit.

Blessing of Safekeeping
Psalm 16; Acts 2:25-33

I bless you, in the Name of Jesus Christ,
   with safekeeping.
Because you have run to God
   and said to Him, *Be my Lord!*
   you enjoy refuge in Him.

I bless you with choosing God,
   first and only—no longer
   living under multiplied sorrows,
   bartering for another god.
In choosing God,
   I bless you with discovering
   that He has already chosen you.

Not only has He chosen you,
   He has made you His heir
   and He is your inheritance.
May you revel in the beauty
   of your heritage.

I bless you with instruction in the night.
The wise counsel of the Lord during the day
   is confirmed in your sleep by night.
Day and night, may you bless the Lord,
   because He is continually before you
   and has taken you by your hand.
You will not be shaken.

I bless you with celebration!
God has canceled your ticket to hell—
    it is no longer your destination.
Jesus was resurrected from the dead,
    bodily, without decay.
You, too, have got your feet on the path of life.
You will experience resurrection life.
I bless your soul with exuberance
    as you revel in the wonder of it all.

May you experience radiance
    coming from God's face—
    His presence filling you with joy,
    His hand holding yours,
    leading you in the right way.
I bless you with the pleasures
    you were created to delight in.

Blessing of Grace
Psalm 67

In the name of Jesus Christ,
    I bless you with radiating
    God's grace and blessing.
May the joy and wonder
    of experiencing the smile of God
    reflect on your countenance.
God is just, and He will guide the nations.
Because you are marked with blessing,
    the whole earth will see
    how God works and saves.
The four corners of the world will honor Him.

Blessing of Sabbath Rest
Psalm 131; Hebrews 4:9-11

*A blessing I wrote for our family before Garris and I entered
a sabbatical.*

In Jesus' Name, I bless you with rest—
    a Sabbath Rest.
I bless you with experiencing God's hand on you.
May you make every effort to enter His rest—
    reaching up and taking hold of Him.
You are blessed as you discover
    that your strength is in the might of God.

You have been weaned in Holy Spirit's arms.
May you develop great, child-like trust—
    calmed and comforted
    as a baby embraced by its mother.
Hope now and always.
Wait for God; hope in God.

You have not been too proud;
    may you keep your feet grounded in humility.
In matters too great or too difficult,
    you have cultivated a quiet heart.
May you put your hope in the Lord,
    now and forever.

May you rest in hope,
    contented and unconcerned.
God's plans and purposes are so great,

He will unfold them at the perfect time and place.
Hope now and always.
Wait for God; hope in God.

Blessing of Refreshing
Psalm 84:4-7

A blessing I wrote for my husband.

In the Name of Jesus Christ,
    I bless you with a deep longing
    to experience God's presence
    and a heart of joy in response
    to the Living God.

You are blessed because you draw
    your strength from God.
You have set your heart on a pilgrimage
    along the King's highway.
May you not settle for anything less.
God dwells in you and walks with you;
    you will not perish on your journey.
Your acts of worship will create a safe passage
    through the wilderness.

You have become a road God travels.
Your lonesome valleys will be transformed
    into springs of sweet waters.
Your weeping will become
    a watering hole of blessings.
The autumn rains will cover your life
    with pools of refreshing.

I bless you as you go from strength to strength,
    meeting with Abba Father face to face.

His presence is a sure promise;
    He is with you always and forever.

Blessing of Free and Light Living
Matthew 11:28

A few years ago, Garris and I celebrated our anniversary with an overnight stay in the mountains outside Ashland, Oregon. During that time, Matthew 11:28 became fresh bread from Heaven to our hungry souls and a word we still carry as we continue to contend for such amazing grace.

Are you tired and worn out?
    I bless you with goodness.
Are you carrying a heavy burden?
Jesus does not place upon you
    anything ill-fitting or chafing.

May you hear God's invitation and longing:

> *Come to me,*
> *get away with me,*
> *learn from me.*
> *Listen and respond.*
> *Come, and you will*
> *recover your life.*

I bless you with living freely and lightly
    in your friendship with Jesus.
May you learn what it means to take a real rest
    as you walk with Him.
May you discover His goodness.

I bless you with seeing how delightful it is

to watch how Jesus does things—
to keep company with Him,
to work with Him.
May you move and live
in the *unforced rhythms* of His grace.

PART II:
BLESSINGS OF DIVINE DESTINY FROM PSALM 23

Psalm 23 impacted me in the year 1981. Garris and I were sent out to plant and pastor our first church. We moved from the dream house we had built and from the community we knew and loved. Garris drove a U-Haul packed with our belongings. I drove our car packed with our children—then five and three years old—and our two cats. We made the journey to Montana, where we did not know a soul. The winters were long and harsh, and the towns and cities were few and far between. In that time of transition, God encouraged me with Psalm 23, engraving it in my heart. I also read Phillip Keller's book, A Shepherd Looks at Psalm 23, *which beautifully reveals how God cares for us, His sheep. The following blessings encourage us to remember how loved we are, and that Love is our divine destiny.*

Blessing of the Good Shepherd
Psalm 23:1

*I wrote most of Psalm 23 as a blessing to a spiritual son and
daughter on their wedding day.*

I bless you, in the Name of Jesus Christ,
    with His all-encompassing care.
The God of the universe planned
    a beautiful relationship with you.
May you experience each day of your journey
    knowing you are His cherished child.
He is your Shepherd,
    and you are the sheep of His flock.
You truly belong to Him
    because He laid down His life for you.
You are the object of His affection,
    created in love, by Love, for love.
You have His utmost attention.
May you always acknowledge your need
    for His meticulous watch over you—
    who better to care for you?

I bless you with a simple, ongoing act:
    that you lay down your right to yourself—
    you are no longer your own.
The Good Shepherd created you,
    chose you, named you.
He bought you and calls you His own.
It is His estimation of you that matters;
    anything else cannot be relied upon.

May you always recognize His claim on you—
 give all to Him,
 follow Him and be guided by Him.
May you recognize His authority
 because you belong to Him.
Be blessed because you do not lack anything
 pertaining to life and godliness.

Blessing of Green Pastures
Psalm 23:2

In the Name of Jesus Christ,
    may you dwell in pastures
    you were designed for
    and created to live in.

Jesus, the Good Shepherd, has led you
    to a land of milk and honey,
    bees and blossoms,
    greenest pastures.
He has prepared this place at great cost,
    tending and cultivating
    an environment of rest.
He has planted His Word
    and watered you with the dew
    and rain of His presence.
He satisfies your hunger and thirst.
He handles each detail of your life
    with attentive care.
He longs for you to flourish.
May you satisfy His desire for you,
    having discovered peace and plenty.

Despite your fears, insecurities, stubbornness,
    bad habits, or rebellion, you discover:
    Jesus is not disgusted with you,
    Jesus is not fed-up or angry with you,
    Jesus is not helpless to come to your aid.

He delights in caring for you.
He pours out His unlimited compassion
    and genuine tenderness,
    always working on your behalf.

In spite of trouble, adversity, and opposition,
    you will not struggle alone,
    nor is He indifferent to your pain and hardship.
Nothing takes Him by surprise.
Through every distress and disappointment,
    He is with you. Do not fear.

I bless your spirit, mind, and body
    with vitality and vigor,
    with health and well-being—
    sourced from the water of the Spirit.
You are blessed when you thirst for righteousness,
    and you will be satisfied.
I bless you with the dew of the morning,
    refreshed and revived, contented and at rest
    as you meditate and commune with God.

Drink deeply from the fountain
    of living waters, from the well of the Spirit
    that will never run dry.

Only the Spirit of God
    can satisfy your thirsty soul.
May your thirst be quenched.
I bless you with refreshment
    beside still pools.

Blessing of Renewal

Psalm 23:3

I bless you, in the Name of Jesus Christ,
　　with a restored soul:
　　if you are hopeless and helpless,
　　if you are vulnerable to attack,
　　if you experienced defeat,
　　if you have fallen to temptation,
　　if you have bitterness of soul,
　　if you are distressed and without strength.

I bless your soul with renewal.
The Good Shepherd comes with tenderness
　　no matter where you are.
To reassure you,
　　He comes to pick you up—
　　He comes to rescue you.

He comes to love you as your Father:
　　to discipline you if needed,
　　to keep you from settling for second best,
　　to extend severe mercy in emergencies.

His goal is to restore you.
I bless your soul with restoration.

Your Shepherd will herd and guide you
　　onto safe paths.
He will keep nudging you forward,
　　to fresh pastures.

If left to yourself,
>   you will stick in the same rut,
>   or go around the mountain again and again,
>   without hope of change.

If left to yourself,
>   you will take any appealing route,
>   even if it leads to polluted puddles of disease
>   and ravines of disaster.

If left to yourself,
>   your own behavior will destroy you,
>   and you will not finish well.

Guard against going your own way.
I bless you with deep longings
>   to follow the Good Shepherd.
May you flourish mightily
>   under the wise care of Jesus.
He will keep you moving forward
>   over ground He has already surveyed.
He knows where you will thrive.
He knows every advantage awaiting you.
He brings joy into each new pasture.

I bless you with renewed living.

Blessing of Presence
Psalm 23:4

I bless you, in the Name of Jesus Christ,
    with an awareness of His presence
    as you trek through the valleys
    on your way to new heights.
I bless you on this journey with the flock,
    traveling by day and resting at night,
    under the special attention
    of the Good Shepherd.

He has gone before you and knows
    every detail of your journey—
    nothing will take Him by surprise.
He is fully prepared to keep you safe,
    tending you with skill in every circumstance.
On this rough, wild, and sometimes treacherous trail
    through the valleys, you will not fear.
The Shepherd is beside you:
    when you go through trials,
    when you face death,
    when your heart breaks,
    when you are distressed,
    when the storm is fierce.

You can find refreshing water all along the way;
    green forage is richest on this route.
May you quench your thirst
    and satisfy your hunger.
Even in the darkest valley,

I bless you with strength and courage
and a stronger belief
that you are being led to a good place.
I bless you with reaching higher ground with God.

May you experience the power and protection
of the Shepherd's rod:
an extension of His arm,
a symbol of His strength,
an instrument of discipline and correction.

I bless you with an outpouring of comfort,
safeguarded by the Shepherd,
who wields His rod with expertise,
defending you under threats of danger.

May you love the authority of His rod—
His written and spoken Word,
the extension of His thoughts,
His will and His intentions towards you.

Continue your journey with an open life,
allowing His Word to search your heart,
lighting up and exposing any hidden danger.
The Good Shepherd has compassion
for your well-being.

May the Shepherd's staff bring consolation.
He will lift you up. He will guide you.
He will draw you near to Him—
carefully, gently, skillfully.

You are blessed by His tender heart;
     He desires to lead you on the right path.
You can trust Him and rely on His wisdom
     to assist you for every decision.
Ask and listen for the Spirit's instructions.

I bless you with belonging—
     belonging together with the flock,
     belonging together with Him.

Blessing of Overflow
Psalm 23:5

I bless you, in the Name of Jesus Christ,
 with upgrades of the Spirit.
The Good Shepherd has gone ahead of you,
 to your destination
 on the high mountain range.

He prepares the flat tabletops for dining—
 He is alert to every possible danger,
 He searches diligently for any trouble,
 He will cope with every detail.

The Shepherd is aware of the constant threat
 from the one who comes to steal and destroy.
May you stay close to Him.
I bless you with feasting and celebration,
 even in the presence of your enemy.

The Shepherd imparts the healing
 and anointing oil of His Spirit,
 to bring relief from the abrasive elements of life.
He brings quiet and rest in the face of tension,
 serenity and calmness in the face of frustration,
 strength and well-being despite trouble.

The Shepherd is always active on your behalf.
May your fears shrink and shrivel.
I bless you, in the Name of Jesus Christ,
 with mountain-top experiences,

with adventure,
with peace and tranquility,
with an overflow of goodness.

Blessing of Pursuit
Psalm 23:6

I bless you with full awareness
　　of your identity—you belong
　　to the Good Shepherd.
In the Name of Jesus Christ,
　　receive faith,
　　receive hope,
　　receive love.
God is chasing after you with kindness;
　　Beauty and Love are following you.
May God's goodness overwhelm you;
　　may you be undone by His tender mercies.

I bless you with the reality
　　of an unfathomable truth:
　　the God of the universe pursues you
　　to protect you,
　　to care for you,
　　to prosper you.

You belong to Him,
　　and you will dwell with Him forever!

PART III:
BLESSINGS FROM ISAIAH 49

This chapter tells of the prophecy concerning the Messiah, Israel, and the Church. God spoke Isaiah 49 to Garris, for our family, during a ministry trip we took to Greece in 1999. It was also a word for our transition back to the United States, as well as for the Church. We have carried this prophecy for all these years, and it continues to unfold in the different stages and seasons. We continue to declare God's proclamation through the prophet Isaiah. There is a lot more to come in its fulfillment!

Blessing of Assignment
Isaiah 49:1-3

In the Name of Jesus Christ,
    I bless you with inheritance.
You were given an assignment from God
    the day you were born.
When you entered this world, He named you.
He called you from your mother's womb.

I bless you with rising up and walking
    in the fullness of your destiny—
    glorifying God and fully enjoying Him
    always and forever—
    as you grow in intimacy and oneness with Him.
I bless you with the fulfillment of your calling
    to complete the work
    God has planned for you on the earth,
    and to make your contribution to His Kingdom.
May you keep destiny and calling in the right order—
    may the fruit of destiny inform your calling.

God gave you a voice to be heard—
    anointed speech to cut and penetrate,
    to pierce the darkness.
I bless you with finely-tuned ears
    to hear what the Spirit is saying
    and a trained voice to speak the heart,
    intent, and truth of the Father.
I bless you with words sharper
    than a two-edged sword—

sharp enough to separate bone from marrow
and discern good from evil.
May you choose good.
May you yield any demand you made
for others to hear and understand you.
I bless you with reliance on God's favor
to give you a voice and an audience.

I bless you with God's weighty glory.
May you step under His mighty hand.
He imparts, anoints, empowers, and blesses you.
He keeps His hand on you to protect you.
He conceals you in the shadow of His hand;
He hides you like an arrow in His quiver,
ready to be shot out on assignment
for the Kingdom.
I bless you with receiving God's proclamation
that you are His.
I bless you with hearing His words
pronounced over you:
I will shine through you.
I bless you with intentional,
ongoing, yielding, submitting,
and whole-hearted dependence upon God.
May you reflect Him brilliantly.

Blessing of Marvelous Design
Isaiah 49:4-7

In the Name of Jesus Christ,
I bless you with revelation and reception
    concerning your birth and life.
From the womb you were created in love,
    by Love, for love.
You were created and formed
    in the joyous laughter of the Trinity.
God designed you marvelously.

You were created for assignments too big for you—
    impossible to accomplish in your own power.
God set you up as a light for the nations
    so that His salvation goes global!
I bless you with living in the honor
    bestowed upon you—
        that God be your strength.

You have said:

> *I've worked for nothing.*
> *I have nothing to show*
> *for a life of hard work.*

It appears to you that little has been accomplished
    and your work has been in vain.
You have been kicked around and bullied,
    used, abused, and despised.
You dreamed and struggled for so much more,

expending what now seems like wasted energy.
I bless you with hearing what God has to say
    and with receiving due justice from Him.

God has chosen you,
    and He is faithful to His Word.
The light shining through you
    will draw others to Him.
Leaders, rulers, and nations will kneel before Him.
May your response be:

> *I will let God have the last word;*
> *I will let God pronounce His verdict.*

I bless you with God's reward.

Blessing of Safety
Isaiah 49:8-13

In the Name of Jesus Christ,
    I bless you with discernment of the times.
When the time is ready, God answers you.
He declares:

    In a favorable time, when victory is due,
    I will help you. I formed you and destined you
    for such a time as this.
    I will keep you and strengthen you.

I bless you with responding
    to God's plan for deliverance—
    seeing His hand bring order
    to what has been ruined.
He will keep you safe, resettle you, reestablish you,
    and give you your heritage.
Where you are imprisoned—
    bound and huddled in fear—
    hear your call to freedom:
    It is safe. Come on out and be free.

I bless you with receiving Abba's provision.
May you be filled with fullness from Him—
    your thirst quenched and your hunger satisfied.
I bless you in all areas of barrenness.
May you discover provision
    in the most unlikely places.
I bless you with reviving shade from the sun

and shelter from the wind

The Compassionate One is guiding you.
He is leading you to the best springs.
He is making a way for you—
    turning mountains into roadways.
The trail that has been a difficult,
    slow, uphill climb,
    God will turn into a highway.
I bless you with sped-up resolutions and arrivals.
Be encouraged knowing that God will not delay.
He is waiting for you.

You have been raised up
    to be used by God,
    to call others into freedom
    and inheritance.
I bless you with anointed words
    and supernatural gifts
    to bring people out of darkness,
    into light and safety.
May you fulfill your assignment
    to reconnect people with God—
    to help build super-highways
    for people streaming back
    from isolation and exile.

I bless you with seeing from Heaven's viewpoint.
God is building and rebuilding you.
Those who destroyed and devastated you
    will be gone.
Let the Heavens celebrate and the earth come alive!

Where you have been beaten up,
    God is nursing you tenderly.
Where you are beaten down,
    God comforts your bereaving heart.

Blessing of Hope
Isaiah 49:14-16

In the Name of Jesus Christ,
    I bless you with turnaround in your perceptions.
Where you feel confused and alone,
    as though God has left you,
    or that He has forgotten you even exist,
    I bless you with a shaft of light and truth.
You are always before Him
    and continually upon His heart.
I bless you with the comfort of Holy Spirit's care:
    your cuts and wounds, tended—
    your bruises, healed.

God declares:

> *Can a mother forget her nursing child?*
> *Can she walk away from a baby she bore?*
> *Is it possible she would not have any compassion?*
> *Even if a mother can forget her child,*
> *I could not forget you—ever.*
> *Look, I have written your name*
> *on the back of my hand.*
> *I've never taken my eyes off you.*
> *I especially oversee the restoring of anything broken.*
> *I watch carefully over you.*

I bless you with basking in the gaze of your Creator.
He is especially tending
    to what you consider faulty and worthless.

When you feel hopeless and helpless,
    He longs for you and waits for you to turn to Him.
When you believe you are forever tainted and ruined,
    He washes you completely and covers you.
When you are invalidated and abandoned,
    He is forever before you—face to face.

He has never taken His eyes off you;
    He does not turn away in disgust.
He does not wait until you get your act together
    to get close to you.
May your self-protected heart—a heart
    determined to not be shamed again, ever—
    see Jesus sitting with you in your mess,
    with His arms around you,
    inviting you to life.
You are God's treasure and delight.

Blessing of Spiritual Sight
Isaiah 49:17-26

In the Name of Jesus Christ,
Look up and look well!
    I bless you with amazement and wonder.
What you thought you had lost—
    heritage, hopes, and dreams,
      family and friends, land, and possessions—
    they are being gathered…
    do you see them coming to you?
You lost everything and had nothing.
You were cut off without a place to call home.
Your broken heart was buried in grief.
Look up, and see!

Like discovering a lost treasure of great value,
    be blessed with wonder and delight.
Like an invitation to a wedding,
    may you respond with great celebration.
Remaining comfortless
    will not protect you from further injury.
May you accept His love and joy in you.
I bless you with receiving back
    the treasure you lost
    and wearing it like jewels made for a bride.
I bless you with receiving God's provision
    and protection, as your enemies
    become a fading memory.
I bless you with surprises of the Spirit.
What seems impossible is possible for God.

I bless you with hearing the Word of the Lord:
    He is your double portion—
    more restored to you than what you lost.
I bless you with seeing your children coming home—
    even the children you did not know you had.
What was devastated and decimated will be restored,
    with not enough room to hold all the goodness.
May you stand and stare in wonder
    as you ask yourself how this could be.

I bless you with these words from the Master:

    You will know that I am God.
    Those who wait in hope
    will not be put to shame.
    You will never regret waiting in hope.

May you entrust yourself
    to the One who is true to His word.
I bless you with retrieving what was stolen.
Can anyone be rescued from a tyrant
    who imprisoned, enslaved, and victimized them?
Especially if that someone has great authority
    and power? Even so—even if all odds
    are against you, God declares:

    I am the One who is on your side.
    I am the One who defends your cause.
    I am the One who rescues your children.

PART IV:
BLESSINGS FROM THE
BOOK OF ZECHARIAH

Zechariah means "Yahweh Remembers," and he is one of the most messianic of all the Old Testament prophets. He faithfully prophesies the message God gives him, including God's words of the end-times. The passage that first caught my attention and comforted me was the call to rebuild the Temple—my life—by the ministry of the Holy Spirit...not by human power and might (Zechariah 4:6). Holy Spirit would remove every obstacle that stood against me in the rebuilding and restoration.

Blessing of Trust
Zechariah 1:3

In the Name of Jesus Christ,
   I bless you with ears to hear the Father's invitation:
   Come back to me!
If you have determined that there is no way back,
   and you are stuck with your history....
If you believe you have no choice but to settle for less,
   and don't deserve a second chance....
If you have decided to go your own way,
   believing no one is there for you....
If so, I bless you with illumination in your darkness.

God is the Creator of the world.
He is the Creator of love;
   He knows how to love well.
He chose to love you—
   He chose people who made mistakes,
   He chose people who failed,
   He chose people who were not successes,
   He chose people who were weak,
   He chose people who often did not choose Him.
He chose people to love them
   the way He loves Jesus.

May you repent of choosing unbelief;
   may you choose courage to trust.
I bless you with the revelation
   of God's kind intentions towards you.
Is anything too much for God?

Is your case too hard?
God has spoken:

> *Come back to me,*
> *so I can come back to you.*

He feels distant because of barriers you have erected;
   He has never left you.
I bless you with hearing the Word of the Lord.
May you respond to His invitation
   without hesitation.

Blessing of Awe
Zechariah 2:5, 8, 10-13

I bless you with the manifest presence of God;
    He is right there with you.
He has decreed:

> *I will be a ring of fire surrounding you,*
> *forming a wall of protection.*
> *I will be a radiant presence in your midst.*

I bless you with glorious light;
    may His brilliance overcome you.

I bless you with a holy awe—
    God is on the move!
May you shout and celebrate!
He is your breakthrough.
He has spoken:

> *You are the apple of my eye.*
> *Anyone who hits you,*
> *blackens my eye.*
> *Those who contend with you,*
> *contend with me.*

Silence everyone;
    may you stand in hushed wonder.
God is on the move!

Blessing of Deliverance
Zechariah 3:1-2, 7

I bless you with songs of deliverance
    as you are stripped from all your sin—
    washed and clothed.
I bless you with newness of life.
When Satan stood against you in accusation,
    God rebuked the accuser and chose you.
He pulled you from the fire.
May your song of celebration be heard
    to the far reaches of the world!

I bless you with the life God intended for you—
    living the way He tells you to live,
    in responsive obedience.
You are destined to govern with His authority—
    making decisions and overseeing His affairs.
I bless you with wisdom and revelation
    that will influence nations and shift cultures.

Blessing of Yes
Zechariah 4:6-9

I bless you with God's decree
>as you encounter anyone who opposes Him
>and whatever stands against His Word:

Who do you think you are?
You may be a great mountain,
and yet you are nothing but a molehill
in the eyes of God.

I bless you with revelation of God's plan for you.
May you move and act
>in the might and power of the Holy Spirit.
Rather than operating from your own power source—
>trying to force results—
>may you partner with Abba, Father.
Hear and do what He says and does.

I bless you with trust in the might of God,
>refusing burdens not meant for your hands,
>yielding the weight of outcomes
>without control and manipulation.
May you renounce your demand
>for performance by the sweat of human ingenuity.
Instead, may you respond with *Yes! Yes!*
>*Spirit of God, do what only you can do!*
May you shout, *Grace! Grace!* to every problem,
>proclaiming God's favor.

All of God's promises in Christ Jesus are *Yes!*
You are authorized to extend His Kingdom,
    to decree His will,
    to make Him famous.
May you declare *Yes*
    in agreement with the *Yes* of God.
Yes to the promises recorded in the Word of God,
    yet to be fulfilled.
Yes to ongoing promises available by faith.
Yes to prophetic revelation through God's voice
    and the gifts of Holy Spirit.

I bless you with a new mindset and response
    to "impossibilities,"
    to issues too large and difficult,
    to assignments beyond your talent and gifting,
    to unreachable dreams,
    to doors locked shut.
May you entrust yourself to God
    despite what appears to be unattainable.
In the Kingdom of God,
    every negative has a positive,
    every problem has a promise and provision.

I bless you with trust in God's resources.
May you build and sustain your life by His Spirit,
    not by sheer prowess, wealth, or human virtue—
    you can't force these things.

God reminds you:

    It's not by your might

or by your strength —
but by my Spirit.

Take hold of promise and provision;
   be blessed with an outpouring of favor.

Blessing of Completion
Zechariah 4:10

I bless you in each step of the process.
Do not despise small beginnings.
God is watching over His Word
  to confirm and perform it.
He has created the design,
    He has laid the cornerstone and foundation,
    He is building the *structure*.

I bless you with His work of completion
    as you grow in intimacy with God
    and fulfill His call on your life.

Blessing of Cultural Transformation

Zechariah 6:12-13

In the Name of Jesus Christ,
    may you partner with Him
    as His representative.
May you walk in your spiritual inheritance.
I bless you with God's anointing
    as you serve in your priestly role
    of petition and intercession,
    and offering up prayer and worship
    with grace and mercy and love.

I bless you with stepping into your kingly role.
May you represent God's authority to people,
    releasing His rule from Heaven to earth,
    decreeing His decisions and orders,
    declaring what He has stated and announced.
I bless you with proclaiming the Word of the Lord,
    as inspired by Holy Spirit.

May you rise up in your royal priesthood
    to take the keys of Kingdom authority
    and fully shift earthly governments.
May you boldly decree God's Word
    and live in the release of His extraordinary power.

Blessing of Justice
Zechariah 7:8-14

In the Name of Jesus Christ,
    may you be receptive to God's desire for you.
He is just and He created you to love justice
    and to be just.
He desires that you be treated justly.
I bless you with true justice.

For any who would take advantage of you,
    plot or scheme against you,
    may their hearts be softened,
    their stubbornness and anger repented.
May justice be extended to you.

I bless you with experiencing God's grace.
Because of the favor you walk in
    may you, in turn, extend that grace to others
    and to wherever you put your hand.

I bless you with so much favor,
    that injustice turns to justice.
I bless you with a double portion in return
    for whatever was lost or stolen.

When God calls out for justice
    and people do not listen,
    He waits for them to turn back to Him.
Without Him, they become scattered
    like leaves in a wind storm.

They will experience desolation in their land;
    their own judgment comes back upon their heads.
I bless you with courage and patience
    toward those who have inflicted
    wounds of injustice.

I bless you with responding in the opposite spirit,
    treating each other justly,
    acting in love and compassion.
May mercy triumph over judgment.
I bless you with a heart of forgiveness
    and reconciliation.

In the Name of the Lord Jesus Christ,
    I command that all strongholds
    associated with injustice be torn down.
I renounce any authority given to the enemy—
    spirit, soul, and body.
I take that authority back.
I break all curses stemming
    from abusive words and actions,
    rendering them powerless, null, and void.
I declare freedom that births freedom in others.
May you experience the joy of dancing upon injustice.

Blessing of Ease
Zechariah 8:2-8

In the Name of Jesus Christ,
    I bless you with an open, receptive heart
    to the relentless, pursuing, zealous love of God
    who declares:

    I care about you!
    I'm involved in your life!

May you become permeated with wonder
    in the knowledge of His indwelling presence.
Abba has given you a new name;
    He has renamed your dwelling Truth.
He has made you a habitation of holiness.
He has turned your home into a place of goodness.
    I bless you with playfulness and laughter,
    because you dwell in safety.

The Lord speaks:

    Do problems seem too much?
    Is anything too much for me?
    Nothing is too hard if I have my say.
    I will bring back the prodigals.
    I will bring back the lost and forgotten.
    I will bring home those who have wandered off.
    I will bring them back and move them home.

I bless you with a family reunion!

May you delight in God's proclamation:

> *You will be my people,*
> *and I will be your God.*
> *I will be with you,*
> *in righteousness and truth.*

I bless you with ears to hear:
    you are His,
    and He is yours.
He will always be with you.
He will always do right by you.

Blessing of Good News
Zechariah 8:9-17

In the Name of Jesus Christ,
    I bless you with the Word of the Lord.
May you have ears to hear
    what He is saying through His prophets.
Hold tight and be strong.
As the dwelling place of God,
    you are being reestablished,
    you are being rebuilt.

You have come through a hard time.
You have worked for little and not had enough.
Peace has been a rare commodity,
    with danger all around.
You could not let your guard down;
    you have not felt safe.
May you hear these words from the Lord:
    I have changed your reality.

I bless you with everything you need—and more!
The sowing and harvesting will resume;
    grapes will hang on the vines.
The dew and rain will paint the landscape green,
    yielding produce and plenty.

Any bad news is no longer your heritage—
    you are now the Good News people,
    you have become a blessing.
Don't be afraid; God has saved you.

I bless you with keeping a firm grip
    on what He is doing.

May you become even more of a blessing.
False and even vicious judgments against you
    cannot have a hold on you.
Your higher reality is not dishonor.

Those who have taken unfair advantage of you—
    saying or doing what is not true—
    they will ultimately be found out.
May you, however, be the bearer of truth;
    speak the truth—the whole truth—in love.

Blessing of Being a Marvel
Zechariah 8:18-23

In the Name of Jesus Christ,
    I bless you with a love for truth and peace.
May your days of sorrowful mourning
    turn to days of joy and gladness,
    to holidays of celebration.
May you embrace truth and love peace!

May you be a marvel of God's goodness.
People and their leaders will hear your Good News
    and desire to get in on God's blessings.
Because of you, leaders will come to a conclusion:

> *What is keeping us*
> *from praying to the Lord of Hosts?*
> *Shouldn't we also seek*
> *the favor of God?*

I bless you with great influence for the Kingdom—
    powerful nations with many people
    speaking different languages, coming to you,
    looking to get a blessing from God.

May you experience a ten-fold impact—
    people approaching you, grabbing your sleeve,
    asking if they can go with you.
Because of God's marvels,
    strangers are seeking you out and saying to you:
    We have heard that God is with you.

Blessing of Beauty
Zechariah 9:9-17

In the Name of Jesus Christ,
    I bless your encounters with the King.
He is a good King who makes all things right.
He is both humble and mighty,
    and He has come to you!

Because of His blood covenant with you,
    be filled with hope.
He has set you free;
    He restores everything you lost.
No longer are you a victim.
You are now a beautiful weapon:
    a pulled bow, a warrior's sword,
    in the hands of God.

You are blessed with His shepherding protection,
    carefree like a flock of soft, gentle lambs.
The King has saved the day;
    He has rescued you!
He has made you like precious gemstones in a crown,
    catching the colors of the sun,
    sparkling with brilliance,
    shimmering and glowing.
I bless you with His beauty.

Blessing of the Rain of the Spirit

Zechariah 10:1; James 4:2

A scripture spoken over us by Dick Mills in 1993.

I bless you, in the Name of Jesus Christ,
    with renewal, reformation, and revival.
Ask the Lord for rain—and keep asking—
    so that the land will prosper.
I bless you with a double portion of rain,
    an outpouring from the Rainmaker,
    not only as your blessing
    but to be a blessing for others.

A supernatural outpouring began
    on the day of Pentecost
    and continues increasing
    until the end of the age
    when Jesus returns.
Ask for more of the reality of the Kingdom.
You are not begging as though you are an orphan—
    your request has already
    been made available to you.
God is not holding back His blessing
    and then relenting because of your efforts.
Partner with Holy Spirit and get ready.
I bless you with participation.

I bless you with an awakening to your full inheritance.
Receive what has been given to you;
    may you respond with *yes* to more!

It is not because you are greedy that you ask.
God wants you to want more of His manifest presence
    and not settle for less.
Your intense cry for more is not from a place of lack
    but from the wealth and sufficiency of Jesus Christ.

I bless you with a desire
    for the great abundance already given.
Jesus demonstrated the Kingdom.
The early Church moved in power;
    it was a force to be reckoned with—
    deliverance, healing, and the dead raised to life.
May you see what has already been made available—
    more character of the fruit of the Spirit,
    more power of the gifts of the Spirit.
From glory to glory, He is changing you.
I bless you with a deluge of rain.

> *Ask me. You do not have*
> *because you have not asked.*
> *You are in need, but you*
> *have stopped contending*
> *for the promise. Get ready.*

Blessing of Homecoming
Zechariah 10:3-11

In the Name of Jesus Christ,
    I bless those of you who have wandered—
    comfortless and afflicted—
    without a shepherd.
God will step in and care for you.
I bless you with fresh water
    and green pastures.
Be revived in your spirit.

May you fulfill your purpose and destiny,
    proud to be on God's side,
    fighting His battles, courageous and strong,
    undeterred because He is with you.
You will not be put to shame.

God will use you in His work of rebuilding.
The Messiah is the cornerstone, the tent peg;
    He is the ruler over all.
The destiny of humankind hinges on Him.
May you be the foundations and pillars,
    the tools and instruments,
    to oversee His work.
I bless you with strength and deliverance
    because of the Lord's compassion for you.
He is your God and He will answer you.

The Lord knows your pain;
    may you discover His good plan for you.

He will make you as good as new.
    He has given you a fresh start,
    as if nothing bad had ever happened.
The Lord declares:

> *I am your very own God;*
> *I will do what needs*
> *to be done for you.*

I bless you with a testimony of God's goodness:
    your life brimming with joy,
    your overflow pouring upon your children
    who get in on it, too—
    may they be blessed by God!
Your story will stay alive
    and be remembered.

I bless your children's journey
    as one marked by a homecoming.
Despite troubled seas
    and roaring rivers of distress,
    God will bless your children with life—
    He will bring them home.

I bless your children
    with the strength of the Lord,
    with living God's way,
    with walking in His name.

PART V:
BLESSINGS FROM THE BOOK OF HABAKKUK

I first encountered Habakkuk as God's written and spoken word to me during a time when someone dear to my heart lost his way. Despite all of my intercession, matters continued to worsen for him. The hymn in the last verses became my story and my song.

Blessing of Standing Firm

Habakkuk 1:1-4

I bless you, in the Name of Jesus Christ,
    with continual faith, even when
    you continually stare trouble in the face.
I bless you with hope in seemingly hopeless places,
    even when you have to look upon evil—
    the weak and helpless mistreated,
    righteous decisions overturned,
    internal problems filled with anarchy and violence.
Even while you cry out to God for justice and order,
    may you stand firm.

Blessing of Tenacity
Habakkuk 1:4-17; 2:1

I bless you with faith when bad gets worse,
    when your questions lead to more questions,
    and the answer you hoped for does not come.
You have witnessed strife and contention.
Injustice forms a passageway for fierce enemies
    who are like relentless winds blasting
    across the land, overrunning
    everything in their path.

You ask:

> *How can more problems*
> *solve the problem?*
> *How can God let this go on?*
> *What is God going to say*
> *to all my questions?*
> *How is He going to answer my complaint?*
> *What will my answer be to His response*
> *when He corrects me?*

May you stand firm and await your answer from God.
    Wait. Be still. Listen.

Blessing of Faith
Habakkuk 2:1-4

As you wait, I bless you with faith.
May you entrust yourself to God;
    the just will live by faith.
Those who are arrogant—
    who attempt to find life in themselves—
    are unstable.

I bless you with trusting God for your life;
    in Him, you will be found dependable and reliable.
You are in right standing before God.
May you be loyal and steady in your belief.

When you ask God what to do, He answers:

    Write the promise, making it plain;
    record the vision to be easily and quickly read.
    Keep it before your eyes, and ensure
    that it will be passed on to the next generation.
    The message points to what is coming.
    The vision will not fail; it will not lie.
    Though it seems slow to come, wait for it.
    It will certainly come, and right on time.

I bless you with living fully—faith-filled living—
    flourishing and joyful,
    in regenerative health,
    with happiness and gratefulness.

You have been made righteous.
May you be found faithful,
    consistent, and steady in your belief.
You will live!

Blessing of Glory
Habakkuk 2:5-3:16

I bless you with awareness of God's glory
    filling the earth.
God will make sure that injustice
    comes to nothing.
Your Messiah will be your salvation.
Those who are full of themselves, living it up—
    victimizing, grabbing, and looting—
    have undermined their own foundation.
In ruining others, they have ruined themselves.
Their moral weaknesses will lead to their defeat.

God is in His holy Temple!
Listen! May you fall on your knees in holy silence!

I bless you in remembering the greatness of God.
Injustice cannot stand before His splendor.
Remember this as you await deliverance
    from intolerable situations—
    as you await the final resolution.
May you discover your source of hope and joy
    in God—not in your circumstances.
You can count on His mercy.
I bless you with faith in God.

Blessing of Prophecy
Habakkuk 3:17-19

I bless you with a new measure of faith –
    may you truly and fully live,
    may this be your story and song:

    Even though there are no blossoms on the fig trees,
    and there is no fruit on the vines—
    though the olive trees fail to yield
    and the wheat fields produce no food—
    though the cattle barns and sheep pens stand empty,
    God's rule will prevail.
    I will joyfully sing to God!
    I will joy in the God of my salvation.
    The sovereign Lord is my strength.
    I will take heart and grow stronger,
    running like a deer on the mountain tops.
    God will get me to my high places.

Be blessed in the waiting;
    wait for the fulfillment of God's promise.
Be blessed with His wisdom and knowledge
    in understanding the times and seasons.
I declare God's appointed time;
    He will not delay.
May the meditations of your heart
    and the words you speak
    reflect promise.

PART VI:
BLESSINGS OF
RESTORATION

These blessings represent the extravagant love of the Trinity. Jesus spoke these parables from several vantage points: a father (the Father), a shepherd (Jesus), and a mother (Holy Spirit). I expanded them and wrote them as the following blessings.

Blessing from the Father
to the Prodigal
Luke 15:11-24; Romans 8:37-39

In the Name of Jesus Christ,
 I bless you with Abba Father's Love.
Be blessed with remembrance:
 remember His words,
 remember His heart,
 remember His truth,
 remember His love.

May you never forget the way back home.
Your independence—your right to yourself—
 brought dishonor and chaos.
Yet no sin separates you from Father's love—
 because of His grace,
 your relationship with Him is never at risk.
In your act of rebellion,
 living in sin and forming judgments,
 you will suffer.
Those choices will bring loss,
 taking you farther than you ever planned,
 even to your ruin.

Punished by others,
 self-punished,
 but not punished by God,
 may you come to your senses.

I bless you with new eyes to see,
    truth that sets you free,
    and a heart to admit your need
    for your Father.

You don't have to prove your love to be loved.
You don't have to strive at being better.
You don't have to sin less to be acceptable.
May you experience Love
    as you humbly yield,
    lay down your rights,
    and come back Home.

I bless you with an awakening
    and genuine repentance.
May you hear and obey.

Your Father is waiting and expectant.
When He sees you coming,
    He runs to you, embraces you,
    kisses you, and covers your shame
    with His robe of righteousness.
He gives you a ring,
    restoring your position in the family.
He places sandals on your feet,
    proclaiming your destiny as His child.

His joy in your return is so overwhelming,
    He cannot contain His emotions.
He calls for a celebration
    and invites family, friends, and neighbors.

You were lost and now you are found.

I bless you with complete restoration!

Blessing from the Father
to the Elder Son
Luke 15:25-32

I bless you with the Father's Love.
I speak to those parts of your heart
     unable to experience an intimate relationship
     with your Father.
Your attempts to do right and attempts to sin less
     only keep you preoccupied with yourself.
You set yourself up to judge those
     you think sinned more than you.
Be forgiven for your pride,
     in the Name of Jesus Christ.

I bless you with a true righteousness,
     evidenced by how you receive your Father's love
     and how you, in turn, love Him—
     how you give and receive love from your brother.
 Receive the touch of your Father's love,
     so that you can know Him,
     so that you can know His intentions,
     so that you can believe Him.

I declare the Father's words over your heart and mind:

     You are my child.
     You have always been my child.
     Everything I have is yours.

I bless you with the enjoyment
    of your inheritance.

I bless you with humility of heart.
Instead of performance,
    instead of attempts at excellence,
    may you trust and love—
    I bless you with *His* excellence.
Jesus, dwelling in you, is the greatest evidence
    of your righteousness.

Do you hear the longing in Father's voice
    as He calls you to the celebration?
May you hear His invitation
    and catch the spirit of festivity—
    the community of family, friends, and neighbors.
Your brother was lost and now he is found.

I bless you with complete restoration!

Blessing from the Shepherd
Psalm 23:1; Luke 15:4-7

Jesus is the Good Shepherd.
When you saw your need to be rescued
 and you cried out to Him,
 He came for you.
In His care, you lack nothing;
 every need is met.
In the Name of Jesus Christ,
 May you follow Him,
 draw near to Him,
 stay close and safe with Him.

I bless you with help
 if you wandered from the flock
 through ignorance, tangled yourself
 in generational iniquity, and are reaping
 the consequences of your choices.
You may have lived in naïve rebellion,
 making false covenants
 in agreement with darkness.
You may have been enticed by curiosity
 and formed ungodly soul-ties,
 binding vows, self-curses, and judgments.
If you got caught in a trap
 and could not get back home—
 if you became confused
 and unaware of lurking danger—
 I bless you with deliverance and true freedom.

Jesus knows you are missing,
    and He places great value on you.
He leaves the rest of the flock to rescue you;
    He finds you.
He places you on His shoulders
    and carries the shame
    and weight of your guilt.
He puts no blame on you.

To be lost or in trouble by your own making
    carries its own consequences.
I bless you with genuine repentance.
Be filled with wonder at His mercy and grace.
You are not only found and rescued,
    you are in for a big surprise.
The Good Shepherd's care for you is so great,
    His joy in your return so profound,
    He cannot contain His emotions—
    His delight spills into overflow.
He calls for a celebration
    and invites friends and neighbors.
You were lost and now you are found.

I bless you with complete restoration!

Blessing from the Holy Spirit
Luke 15:8-10; Matthew 23:37

I bless you with the nurturing heart of God,
 in the Name of Jesus Christ.
If you were carried in your mother's womb
 unwanted, unloved....
If you find yourself living life
 without much joy....
If you live in isolation without much hope,
 believing no one can be counted on,
 and no one will be there for you....
I bless you with tender comfort of the Holy Spirit
 who loves you, teaches you, and helps you.

You may find yourself lost,
 through no fault of your own.
If you have lived through abuse—
 if you consider yourself worthless,
 neglected, forgotten—
 may you experience the embrace
 of the mothering heart of God.
His Spirit covers you,
 like the wings of a mother hen
 protecting her baby chicks.

The act of being lost is traumatizing,
 leaving you with unhealed wounds and scars,
 misinformation and misinterpretations,
 feeling condemned and degraded.
I bless you with deliverance.

If you have ended up in a dark, hidden
        and unclean place,
        Holy Spirit lights a lamp
        and reveals truth that sets you free.
I bless you with genuine repentance.
Be cleansed of all filth;
        the power of shame is broken in the light.
If you feel so unimportant
        that surely no one would search for you,
        you are in for a big surprise!
You belong, you are accepted,
        you are never alone.
Togetherness is your permanent state.

Holy Spirit will not stop until you are rescued,
        with care for you so great,
        with a joy so profound,
        that friends and neighbors will be invited
        to a great celebration.
You were lost and now you are found.

I bless you with complete restoration!

Blessing of Relationship
Matthew 22:37-40; Luke 10:27

*The key to allowing the Father, Son, and Holy Spirit access
to our hearts to experience restoration is profound, simple,
and something that every person can do. An unspoken
question waits in our hearts: "Would I dare risk unlocking
my heart and trust to receive God's love?" How we answer
that will determine whether we will live a shadowy image of
life or truly live. There is no life without relationship.*

I bless you, in the Name of Jesus Christ,
    with the core foundation
    upon which you stand.

Love the Lord your God
    with all your heart,
    with all your soul,
    with all your mind,
    with all your strength.

May you deliberately turn your soul Godward,
    surrendering your heart to the ongoing
    voyage of seeking God.
Be filled and forever sustained.
When you pursue Him,
    you possess the meaning of life.

In order to love God,
    I bless you with allowing God's love
    to touch you.

You are not commanded to love yourself
    or to forgive yourself.
You can only receive.
Practice and become brilliant
    at receiving God's love.

The more you love God, you have:
    a greater capacity to receive from Him,
    a greater capacity to love Him back,
    a greater capacity to receive more love.

When you are a receptacle of God's love,
    you have love to give.
If you cannot receive God's love,
    you cannot possess it,
    and you cannot give what you do not possess.
When you try to love your neighbor as yourself,
    all you have to give
    is what you have received.
May you pour out what you have been given
    and received with utmost generosity.

I bless you with trust in the Living God.
Trust is love—
    you are letting God love you
    when you entrust yourself to Him.
You are well loved, because you trust Him.

I bless you with humility.
Humility is an act of trust in God:
    an acknowledgement of your need,
    and a looking to God for life and its solutions.

Every act of humility is met with grace:
    Humility.
    Trust.
    Love.

    Abide, dwell, stay with God.
    Receive God's love.
    Love God.
    Give God's love to your neighbor.

PART VII:
BLESSINGS FOR REVIVAL

Over the years, Garris and I have experienced personal revivals on many different levels. Jesus is continually reviving His Church at any given moment around the globe. But we are waiting for a revival larger than all past revivals put together. The stage is set. During the Azusa Street Revival a hundred years ago, worldwide revival was prophesied to begin at this time in history. We are preparing. God always invites His Church to partner with Him. I bless you, in the Name of Jesus Christ, with discernment to understand the time and season we have entered—to be awake and alert, to walk closely with God, to love Him and to love His mercy.

Blessing of Life and Light
John 1:5-18

The Light shines in the darkness,
    and the darkness cannot put it out.

In the Name of Jesus Christ,
    I bless you with Life.
The glory of God was released at His word,
    and life came into being—
    it came into existence through Him.
Nothing came into being without Him.
I bless you with Life, Himself,
    who is the Light to live by.
He shines into the darkness;
    darkness cannot extinguish and overcome light.
I bless you with Life and Light.

Jesus is the true Light who enlightens you.
May you entrust yourself to Him.
When you do, you enter Life
    and He brings you into the Light.
May you want Him,
    and may you believe He is
    who He claims to be.
When you receive Him,
    you will be reborn.
I bless you with discovering your true self—
    your identity as a child of God, Spirit-born.

I bless you with a wide, open, receptive heart.

You can receive God's love and life
as a gift from Him.

Created in the image of God and born of God,
you, too, have creative power.
May you transform atmospheres
and speak life into existence by the Holy Spirit.
The glory of God released through you
will overpower the world of darkness.
The power of God's glory
will wipe out any resistance.

Grace and truth were realized through Jesus.
No one had seen a glimpse of God,
but Jesus has made Him plain as day.
May you see God's glory with your own eyes.
I bless you with His bounty—
gift after gift after gift of His generosity
inside and out.
I bless you with God's endless knowledge
and His wisdom—
all given through Jesus, the Messiah.

Blessing of Remembrance
Psalm 22

In the Name of Jesus Christ,
    I speak to you who feel forsaken,
    and I bless you with the revelation of Jesus.
He knows what suffering is;
    He is not untouched by yours.
Like Him, you agonize and cry out:

My God, why have you forsaken me?

You call to Him:

I don't hear an answer from you.
I toss and turn all night without rest.
Yet I remember that others trusted you,
and they were not disappointed.

I bless you with stories of deliverance.
Your testimony is the testimony of Jesus;
    what is true for Him is true for you.
God was the midwife at your birth.
When you left your mother's womb,
    He cradled you.
He has been your God from your conception.
I bless you with new life
    and childlike trust.
May you see Him holding you close.

I speak to your crushed heart—

devoured, dead, and buried—
    I say, "Rise up!"
To your history of abandonment,
    loneliness, separation, and solitude—
    to your experience of being slighted,
    abused, stepped on and squashed—
    I speak, "Resurrection life!"

To your joints that have been pulled apart,
    to your bones that have dried up,
    to the wrenching in the pit of your stomach,
    I declare healing, in Jesus' Name.

I bless you with witnessing goodness.
God has never let you down;
    He has never looked the other way.
He has never left you to do His own thing.
He has been right there—
    even when you were being kicked around.

When others shook their heads at you,
    taunting and jeering:

    If God likes you so much,
    let's see how much He really cares.
    If He really is who He says He is—
    If He really can help you and rescue you—
    then let Him deliver you.

I bless you with experiencing rescue.
May you truly know
    that God has always stood with you and by you.

He has carried the burden of those cruel,
    wounding actions as His own.
Whenever you cried out to Him,
    He has been right there listening to you,
    bearing the magnitude of your grief.

When you felt rejected,
    separate from others, forever alone—
    when a part of your heart
    lived in perpetual darkness—
    when you felt like you were buried alive,
    a fate worse than death—
    may you see Jesus right there with you.
He has experienced the same—and worse.
He has never left you in your journey.
May you see Him,
    feel His arms around you
    hear His heartbeat—
    be touched, healed, loved,
    and forever transformed.

I bless you with sitting at God's table
    and eating until satisfied—
    living in fullness of life.
Because you sought God,
    and you found Him,
    you have discovered a life of praise.

May your acts of worship
    show others the way home.
From the ends of the earth,
    people will start coming to their senses

and running back to God.
Lost families will fall on their faces before Him.
The prosperous will worship Him—
    the poor and powerless will worship,
    as well as those of us who never got it together!

I bless you with a life of worship before God.
I bless you with living out of your godly heritage.
Your children and their children will get in on
    your declarations of God's righteousness.
Even children not yet conceived
    will hear the Good News
    that God will do what He says.
He will perform His Word.
I bless your future generations with salvation.

Blessing of Authority I
Jeremiah 1:10

I bless you, in the Name of Jesus Christ,
    with moving in the King's authority.
May you carry out His decrees,
    destroying and throwing down
    demonic forces who are opposing
    the advancement of the Kingdom of Heaven,
May you root out and pull down
    any establishment of wickedness
    that controls nations, governments,
    and individuals through corruption and greed.
You are not wrestling with people
    but with the forces they are yielded to.
May righteous men and women rise up
    and stand in the gap for you.
May you lead people back to God.
I bless you with building up.
I bless you with planting and bearing much fruit.

Blessing of Authority II
Isaiah 22:22; Matthew 16:18-19; I Peter 2:9

Jesus has given you access to Heaven
    by the shedding of His blood.
In the name of Jesus Christ,
    I bless you with answering God's call
    to Kingdom governance.
May you be His governing force,
    with great favor to influence
    and represent Him and His will.

May you stand securely on the Rock
    upon which you are built.
You are one of many building stones
    called the Church,
    assigned to govern the affairs
    of your family, city, state, or nation.
May you legislate from the spiritual realm.
May you infiltrate your society and alter the culture,
    extending God's Kingdom on the earth.

You have been given keys of authority.
May you walk in kingly intercession,
    shifting the rule, decrees, and councils of hell.
May you fight for justice before God
    on behalf of others.
The gates of Hades—the power of death—
    cannot claim victory over you
    and those who belong to God.
The governmental decisions of hell

cannot prevent the advance of God's Kingdom.

I bless you with appropriating and administrating
    God's keys of authority.
I bless you with closing spiritual doors
    through which destruction and evil
    might otherwise enter.
I bless you with divine strategy
    in the use of your delegated authority.
May you stand on a firm, secure foundation.

I bless you with the gift of discerning of spirits,
    seeing good and evil—and choosing good.
May you use these keys to close spiritual doors,
    disallowing the enemy any legal rights
    to continue affecting you
    and your generational line.
May you rise up an overcomer—no longer a victim—
    as you close, lock, and forbid access from hell,
    as you take captive every thought
    that rises up against the truth
    and knowledge of God.
When God is involved,
    doors that are shut in Heaven
    can be shut on earth—and no one can open them.

Where you have experienced delays and roadblocks,
    I bless you with even greater favor.
May what has been stolen and looted by the enemy
    be delivered back to you—returned with interest!
God has placed victory into your hands,
    freeing you to rebuild what has been destroyed.

He has given you His words to speak.
I bless you with courage to follow Him.
May you experience a shift
　　as your circumstances give way to your words.

I bless you with unlocking doors that are shut.
May you begin by unlocking every door of your heart
　　and allowing access to Jesus.
He stands at the door and knocks.
He longs to be invited in,
　　to break bread with you,
　　to be a protective elder brother for you
　　and a Friend above all friends.
He is your Salvation and Deliverer.

I bless you as you open doors—
　　forbidding lethargy and doubt.
I bless you with the gift of prophecy
　　to declare the heart of God.
Any unfulfilled promise
　　is *yes* in Christ Jesus.

I bless you with hope and fearlessness
　　in the face of powerful strongholds
　　and closed, ancient doors.
Age, size, and strength are irrelevant
　　compared to God's ability to save.
When God is involved,
　　doors that are open in Heaven
　　can be opened on earth—
　　and no one can close them.
The King of Glory will walk through

and His Kingdom will be released.

Not only are you a recipient of blessings,
    you have the authority and favor to bless others.
You are in training to execute matters for the King.
I bless you with His wisdom and grace
    to walk in the heavenly realm of the *possible*.
I bless you with embracing the power given you—
    with hearing what Holy Spirit is saying
    and doing what Holy Spirit is doing in this hour.

May you impart and empower and equip others
    to also take hold of the keys of the Kingdom.
As a righteous steward, may you
    distribute the Father's resources
    from the treasuries of Heaven
    and reveal the mysteries of God.

You have the keys to bring blessings.
May you pray for those who curse you,
    love those who hate you and mistreat you,
    forgive those who offend you,
    give to those in need,
    and walk humbly before God.

Blessing of the Possible
Luke 1:37; Matthew 19:26; Acts 2:7, 12

I bless you, in the Name of Jesus Christ,
    with living in the realm of the possible.

    He has called what is barren, fruitful.
    He has called what is weak, strong.
    He has called what is poor, rich.

Living out of who God says you are
    is your only hope of experiencing
    your true identity—not by
    improving on the old you,
    but by Holy Spirit's indwelling.
What is impossible for you
    is possible with God.
When you come to the end
    of what you can do on your own,
    what you can change,
    what you can work for....
You are ready to face
    what is impossible for you.
You are ready to enter
    what is possible with God.

I bless you with living in a realm
    that is impossible for you,
    but possible for God.
I bless you with:
    favor, glory, reformed beliefs,

and transformed hearts.
I bless you with:
    wisdom, knowledge, prophecy,
    visions, dreams, healings, and miracles.

May people be amazed and astonished
    at an outpouring of the Holy Spirit,
    when they see the mighty works of God.

I bless you in each new day
    with dreaming the "possible of God."

Blessing of Finishing Well
II Corinthians 12:9-10; Zechariah 4:6

In the Name of Jesus Christ,
     may you walk in God's might and power.
Your own strength is never sufficient.
You don't have enough zeal to accomplish the goal.
Sooner or later you will give up—
     you will lose confidence,
     you will stop anticipating
     the fulfillment of the promise.
You cannot maneuver and steer yourself
     into all that your Father has purposed for you.
May you be given the gift of seeing your limitations
     and refusing the luxury of self-hatred.

I bless you with taking your weaknesses in stride.
Instead of focusing on your handicaps,
     may you experience Christ's strength
     moving through your weakness.
When you recognize a weakness, welcome sight;
     sight is the beginning of healing.
When your enemy tries to get you down,
     fall forward into grace.
You are not made weak in order for God
     to look good; you *are* weak—
     you need more love, more hope, more joy.
He is your strength.
I bless you with these words of Jesus:

     My grace is all you need; it is enough.

In your weakness, my strength is displayed.

I bless you with God's power to finish well:

Not by your own might or strength
but in the power of the Holy Spirit.

Blessing of Revival
Amos 9:11-13

We are in the midst of the ongoing fulfillment of Amos'
prophecy, written in 760 BC regarding the Messiah, Israel,
and the Church. The initial fulfillment began at the birth of
Jesus and will be completed at the end of the Age. This
prophecy has been an ongoing theme and influence in our
lives.

I bless you, in the Name of Jesus Christ,
    with His plan of redemption for you.
I bless you with hope as you survey
    what is broken down and in disrepair.
God is in the business of rebuilding what has fallen
    and repairing the damages.
I bless you with settling it in your heart,
    once and for all, that God is good.
Death and destruction are in opposition to God.
He is leading you out of lack,
    depression, and hopelessness
    into a good place.

I bless you with immense blessings—
    blessings like abundant crops in the land
    that produce so quickly and so richly,
    it is difficult to finish one cycle of growth
    before the next cycle begins.
Even while one person is plowing
    the land for planting,
    another will already be cutting ripe corn—

so rapidly will the corn grow and ripen.
And the vintage of grapes will be so fruitful,
	the treading will last to the planting time.

May you be filled with awe
	at God's good intentions toward you.
His desire is to bless you—
	and through you, the nations.
God's people are entering another depth
	in this ongoing fulfillment of an ancient prophecy.
Things are speeding up and happening so fast,
	you won't be able to keep up.
Everything will be happening at once—
	everywhere you look, blessings!

I bless you with a multiplication of fruitfulness
	of God's generosity towards you.
Just as the Promised Land flowed
	with milk and honey,
	the hills will melt and dissolve
	into streams of provision and goodness.
Blessings like wine will pour down the mountains.
I bless you with astounding provision
	for your spirit, soul, and body—
	for you, your loved ones, the Church, the land.

I bless you with seeing the return
	of those taken captive and enslaved—
	those lost and forgotten, unknown and outcast.
They will be brought home.
May you experience the same restoration
	in the hidden places of your heart.

Where you have been uprooted and crushed down,
    I bless you with a homecoming.
Where you have become a wasteland,
    I bless you with deep roots and a vintage crop
    in your place of inheritance.
May you plant vineyards and drink your wine;
    plant gardens and eat the fruit.
God's favor is upon you.
In this unfolding prophecy,
    He will make everything right again.

Revival is coming!
Get ready for a massive outpouring
    greater than any other time in history,
    filled with the presence, glory, and power of God
    invading the atmosphere of this world.
Glory will rest upon every tongue,
    every tribe, and every nation.
Deliverance, salvation, healing, and transformation
    will be propelled by God.
He will ignite us!

I bless you with a prepared heart—
    alert and awake.
May you be ready to lay aside weight and worry,
    to choose love over every offense.
I bless you, in this God-appointed season,
    with glorious intimacy
    as you step into God's manifest presence
    and under the waterfalls of His anointing.

Blessing of the Blessed

Psalm 67

In the Name of Jesus Christ,
    be blessed with His mark of grace!
May He cause His face to shine upon you.
May you experience the brilliance of His smile.
Because of God's blessings on you,
    the whole earth will see how He works
    and see how He saves.
Because God has judged fairly,
    great joy and happiness abound.
The nations guided by Him are thankful.
Even the earth's produce will display
    His blessings with exuberance!
You are marked with God's blessings
    so that the four corners of the earth
    will honor Him.
God blesses you.

AFTERWORD:
A WORD OF PROPHECY

As I close this book, I would like to share an experience I had. It came in two parts; the first part was more of a vision and the second part more of an impression with a prophetic element. The interpretation came progressively.

Part I

I saw myself swimming in an ocean, a place I usually would deem out of my depth. I would normally not feel strong enough to keep afloat for very long, and diving below the surface would have been frightening. I thought back on scary ocean excursions in my childhood when I had imagined the things and beings in the water that I could not see.

But in this vision, I experienced the ocean in a vastly different way. The ocean was filled with God's love—as though the ocean was the essence of Love—deep and wide, yet wondrous. If I were to go diving (which I did), I found myself too buoyant. Instead of desperately trying to stay afloat and survive, I longed to dive deep and discover more of this Love. However, I kept bobbing to the surface. Holy Spirit instructed me to use the heavy burdens of worry and frustration as weights—since I was already carrying them—to help me sink. I knew that when I wanted, I could then off-load them to Him.

I kept going down and down. Instead of my environment growing darker the deeper I dove, it grew lighter. Colors brightened—everything glowed in heavenly hues of blue.

At one point, I realized that the more weights I *put on*—including all the burdens of duty, responsibility and good works—the faster and deeper my dive. In my mind, I went through the act of strapping these on, as a conscious acknowledgment that I had already been stumbling around on land barely able to maneuver the weight of it all. At certain points in my life, I had been crushed under the load. My *aha* moment of the vision came when I asked Holy Spirit to identify more weights I was unaware of.

The more I practiced, the less condemned I felt by any weighty burden I discovered. Instead, those burdens became my cue to go diving.

Burdens that had been unbearably heavy on land were almost weightless in the water. In fact, they were not the focal point anymore. Mercy had re-formed me. Now my weakness and my failings were experiencing the touch of grace. At some point in the dive, I would give God all of the weights, especially when I felt His magnetic pull was powerful enough to hold me.

Part II

After that first part of the experience, life went on, and I went "deep sea diving" as often as I remembered to—and sometimes simply to draw near to Abba Father. I began to see a prophetic element for the Church and the season we were entering. I understood that a shift had taken place. The Church was being given an upgrade, particularly in the awareness of our destiny. God's love was dispelling fear of what had once been formidable and out of our depth. The transition was akin to a new birth and rebirth. Repentance and cleansing helped us see God and His mysteries.

We were wondrously designed and engineered, with complex coding in our spiritual DNA, for oneness with our Creator. This design was passed down through all generations. By dwelling—abiding—in His Presence, we will no longer be afraid to live in unfamiliar or frightening environments. We are always surrounded by His love, and He is always inviting us to go deeper.

As I was thinking about all of this, I asked the Lord for more revelation.

A thought come to me of blind fish who regained sight. These fish lived for so long in an environment of darkness, that they adapted and did not develop eyes. But when transferred into a habitat with light, they *could* then develop eyes. The ability to regain sight was embedded in their DNA. Sight was in their design.

I could not recall learning about this, so I did

some research and discovered blind Cave Fish. These fish were originally of the same species as sighted fish, but they had been trapped in caves at some point—caves without light. Living for generations in permanent darkness, these fish completely lost their eyesight and developed apparent scars where their eyes had been. But eyes don't just disappear when they aren't needed; within the DNA of eyes are the permanent instructions to construct themselves. Once moved into lighted waters, some of these fish could adapt to see.

Divine destiny can override eons of spiritual blindness—in a single generation.

God is giving you sight where you have been blind to your destiny. He is giving you new capacities of awareness for Him, for your situation, for your life, and for others. You could not see before. In some cases, spiritual genes were corrupted through your generational line, causing blindness. Other types of blindness came through injury. And since we only see in part, sight also has to be imparted to us.

God is ready to help you develop abilities you never dreamed were coded within you. He is bringing you heavenly visions and encounters with Him that will increase from generation to generation.

I end by blessing you with vision into the supernatural:

May you see Him and His glory
with clarity of wisdom and discernment,
with a brighter, light-filled
environment of the Spirit,
with new perceptions, new gifts,
and new capacities,
with comfort in the unfamiliar,
with rest in the presence—
ready for a new day.

ACKNOWLEDGMENTS

Living Waters Church: I love your hearts and your desire to love God and to love others. I am so glad to be in community with you.

Rich Trees: Your class on the book *Search For Significance* was one of those turning points in my life twenty-five years ago.

Roy Hicks, Jr.: You were my first spiritual parent. You went on to be with the Lord many years ago, but your impact remains. You taught me about the Kingdom of God.

Mom and Dad: Thank you for the rich heritage you passed to me. Dad has already gone home to the Lord, but you both continue to bless me. Thank you for loving me.

My children, Anna and David: I am forever impacted and influenced for the better because God gave you to us. Anna, you are a continual inspiration to me. I trust your heart and the wisdom of God in you. Thank you for writing this *Book of Blessings* with me, hand in hand. I am so grateful for your expertise, not only as a writer but an editor. David, you have been a catalyst from birth in teaching me the Father's heart. You have a calling to be a prophet of hope and mercy. Some of these blessings were inspired by you. I love you both with all my heart.

My husband, Garris: We are one, together. We often say we don't know where one of us ends and the other begins. Even now, forty-two years later, I still feel my heart light up when you walk into the room. I'm looking forward with joy to spending the rest of my days and all of eternity with you.

The Scriptures: I am revived by His Word. I love His word. Declaring the truth and blessings of these Scriptures keeps me fixed on Jesus and the higher reality of His Kingdom.